D1107620

The City of Westminster

The City of Westminster

HEART OF LONDON

Photographs and commentaries by Eric de Maré

Introduction by William Gaunt

B. T. BATSFORD LTD London

First published 1968
© Westminster City Council 1968

Printed in the Netherlands by L. Van Leer & Co Ltd
London and Amsterdam, and bound in Great Britain by
Hazell, Watson & Viney Ltd, Aylesbury, for the publishers
B. T. BATSFORD LTD
4 Fitzhardinge Street London W1

Introduction

To describe Westminster as the heart of London is apposite whether one thinks of it geographically as a central region or in a wider sense as the seat of government and law, the home of royalty, a living record of national history, a great nerve centre of contemporary life. Its renowned buildings and monuments, its churches, palaces, parks and river prospects, its institutions devoted to learning, science and the arts, its diversities of aspect, trade and entertainment, indeed make it a capital within a capital.

THE OLD AND NEW CITY

Westminster became a City in 1540 on the foundation of the episcopal see and though the bishopric lasted only ten years has retained the name of City ever since, this status being constitutionally affirmed by royal charter in 1899. Yet Westminster had by then a thousand years and more of antecedent history. Its name was already established in Saxon times by the monastery church or 'minster', where Westminster Abbey now stands, to the west of the wall-encircled City of London. With no loss of historic ground or association but on the contrary with a large extension, there has been a new City of Westminster since 1965. In that year of momentous change, the reorganisation of London boroughs created an inner ring of twelve, among them being the new Westminster, uniting the old City with the adjacent boroughs of Paddington and St Marylebone. The elevation of the mayoralty to the style and dignity of Lord Mayor has marked the importance of the change.

History and practical advantage alike have made it an harmonious integration. Paddington, a part of the Abbey land until the dissolution of the monasteries and the breaking up of their estates, rejoined Westminster after an interval of four hundred years. The plan of streets and squares has for a long time linked Westminster with Marylebone, which was already part of the West End in the latter half of the 18th century. The course of the great Triumphal Way from Regent's Park to Charing Cross, conception of the master-planner, John Nash, can still be traced in spite of many architectural changes.

The amalgamation has made the new City of Westminster one of the largest of London's twelve inner districts. In monetary terms its wealth of property may be estimated at a rateable value of over £107 million, larger than that of any other administrative area in the country. In amenity each of the three constituents has something to add to the whole. But Marylebone was mainly rural until about 1770 and Paddington until the beginning of the 19th century. It was in the older Westminster that a remarkable evolution began, the related development of church and court, palace and abbey. In Parliament Square and on the Victoria Embankment by the Thames, with the bridges and romantic cluster of buildings that have inspired many a masterpiece of painting, the imagination may travel back through the centuries to the dim and conjectural time when Westminster Abbey was founded.

ANCIENT ORIGINS

What led to the choice of its site, on the patch of firm ground amid marsh that came to be known as Thorney Island, a delta bounded by the outflow of the Tyburn stream into the Thames? Not, it has been supposed, a desire for monastic seclusion, but the selection of a convenient crossing-point where the river was fordable. It can be imagined as already a focus of some activity during the Roman occupation. The existence of a Roman settlement has been shown by the fragments excavated within the Abbey precincts. It is not impossible that, as legend has it, the Church of St Peter, as the Abbey is otherwise known, replaced a temple of Apollo.

Though the date of the Abbey's foundation is unknown it is certain that before the Norman Conquest there existed a great church, a monastery of Benedictine monks with cultivated land reclaimed from the marsh and – significant fact – a royal residence. In this later Anglo-Saxon period, Winchester, the old capital, had become too remote to serve as the royal seat. Westminster, conveniently near to the City of London, was the chosen headquarters of Edward the Confessor, and perhaps of other Saxon kings before him.

Harold 'Harefoot' was buried in the Abbey precincts in 1040. The Confessor was buried in the Romanesque church he had rebuilt between 1050 and 1065, the style of which is roughly suggested in the section of the Bayeux tapestry that shows Edward's funeral procession. In this church his successor, Harold II, last of the native English kings, was crowned in 1066. Thus was initiated the tradition of royal burial and coronation that was to continue down the ages. Anxious to declare the legality of his succession by every act, William the Conqueror, after the defeat and death of Harold, had himself crowned in the Abbey by Aldred, Archbishop of York. The Norman kings kept to the already established seat of government and law-giving. The Palace of Westminster, a name still comprehensively applied to the parliamentary buildings of today, was to be both royal abode and legislative centre for more than five hundred years.

HISTORIC GROWTH

The threads of history remain richly woven in the area

extending from the Thames (its midstream being the City's southern boundary) to Charing Cross, an area on which every period down to the present time has left its visible imprint. Historic vestibule to the Houses of Parliament, Westminster Hall, setting in the past of banqueting and ceremony, of royal courts of justice and many a dramatic state trial, tells by its size of William II's ambitious designs for a Norman palace. To its Norman walls, Richard II's master-carpenter, Hugh Herland, added the hammer-beamed roof that may well be considered the most magnificent work of the kind in Europe. A secular relic of the Middle Ages, now standing alone, is the 14th-century 'Jewel House' in which the royal treasure was stored.

History is concentrated in the buildings around Parliament Square. It is an emotional presence in the great Gothic interior of the Abbey rebuilt under Henry III, as one looks down the perspective of time from the tomb of Edward the Confessor to the grave of the Unknown Warrior, from Henry VII's Chapel, superb alike in its fan-vaulting and its statuary, to the 'silent meeting-place of the great dead' in Poets' Corner. The little neighbouring church of St Margaret's, chapel of the House of Commons, though rebuilt in the 16th century is traditionally a foundation of Edward the Confessor, which would make it in origin nearly as old as the Abbey itself. The continuity of government has its stately symbol in the Victorian Gothic towers and chambers of the Houses of Parliament on the site of the old palace buildings destroyed by fire in 1834.

Tradition and expansion have marched together. The Abbey's monastic school was refounded by Elizabeth I as Westminster School, the monks' dormitory then providing its classroom. The splendid 17th-century Ashburnham House, now part of the school, stands on the site of the Prior's Lodging. The long association with royalty spared the Abbey from the fate of other monasteries at the Reformation, and every age has added to its significance as the national memorial of monarchs, heroes and individuals of genius. Ambitious schemes in the past extended the Palace northwards along the 'street of Westminster' that came to be known as Whitehall in the 16th century. It was a rambling series of buildings in royal use at the time of Henry VIII, including the 'Scotland', residence of the Scottish kings, that was to give its name to the Scotland Yard of modern times. The Banqueting Hall in Whitehall is the beautiful fragment of the classical design by Inigo Jones for the palace projected by Charles I, its ceiling painting by Rubens a magnificent testimony to the king's love of art. The projected extensions now have their outcome in the government offices lining Whitehall, built at various periods from the 17th to the 20th century, gaining the enlivenment of pageantry from the Horse Guards gate where the troop of cavalry originally formed by Charles II is always on duty in the brilliant uniform of the past.

Here are the 'corridors of power' – the Treasury, the Home and Foreign Offices, the War Office, the Admiralty, the various ministries and, set back in the little street built by Sir George Downing about 1680, the famous No. 10, the Prime Minister's town house and meeting place of the Cabinet. Elsewhere but still within the boundaries of Westminster are the Royal Courts of Justice and the repositories of national record. The Law Courts, to use the more familiar name, were removed in the Victorian age from the vicinity of Westminster Hall to the last of the great secular buildings of the 19th century to be built in the Gothic style, begun in 1874 and completed in 1883, majestically marking the City's boundary with that of the City of London. One may see Domesday Book in the Public Record Office in Chancery Lane and, among the testaments contained in the late 18th-century grandeur of Somerset House in the Strand, the will of Shakespeare.

ROYAL PALACES AND ASSOCIATIONS

Though the palace of Whitehall did not survive the 17th century, being finally destroyed by fire in January 1698, Westminster continued to be – as it is today – the place of royal residence. Henry VIII had already established a 'fair mansion and park' in the country property he acquired in what is now St James's, while his plans for Whitehall were in train. The mellow Tudor brick of the picturesque gatehouse of St James's Palace goes back to the year in which he married Anne Boleyn. It is a palace of many memories. Thence Charles I walked bravely to execution. There Charles II was born and thither returned in triumph at the Restoration.

Later royal associations are many in the buildings around: Marlborough House, designed by Sir Christopher Wren for the great Duke of Marlborough, in modern times long the home of Queen Mary; Clarence House, built for William IV as Duke of Clarence, the home of Queen Elizabeth, the Queen Mother; Lancaster House, built for the Duke of York, 1825-9, now serving, after changes of name and function, as a stately place of reception and entertainment for distinguished visitors of state.

The other royal residences have developed informally from country houses. But a few paces across the north-western boundary of the City which extends to the Broad Walk in Kensington Gardens is that most unassuming and domestic-looking of palaces, the Kensington Palace of William III and Mary. Buckingham Palace, the main royal residence of today, was originally built as a country house for the Duke of Buckingham in 1705. John Nash redesigned it for George IV though the Marble Arch he intended as an imposing feature of the front (much disliked by William IV) was removed after further reconstruction to its present site on the edge of Hyde Park, where it now stands in ornamental isolation. There is an air of long tradition in the morning scene in the forecourt of Buckingham Palace, the Changing of the Guard, splendid in colour and rhythm, when the New Guard advances to the sound of drum and fife, the sentries are relieved and posted and the Old Guard marches back to barracks to the stirring strains of the military band.

THE ROYAL PARKS

With the royal palaces are to be associated the royal parks. Buckingham Palace has delightful stretches of trees and lake on either side, its own landscape garden on the west and to the east, St James's Park, the favourite walk of Charles II, a delicate miniature with its gay flowerbeds, exotic waterfowl and the little lake and trees so romantically arranged by John Nash that they seem to become a spacious natural landscape. There is here one of London's most picturesque skylines in the view looking towards William Kent's Horse Guards with the fantasy of spires of Whitehall Court behind its clock-tower.

It is remarkable to think that in Westminster with but one or two street crossings it is possible to walk all the way from the Horse Guards Parade to the Round Pond in Kensington Gardens among trees and stretches of green. On the route is Green Park, once part of the chase where Henry VIII hunted deer, never formally laid out and rural-looking still. Then Hyde Park, also Tudor hunting ground, subsequently the gay and fashionable resort for all London it remains. The *Route du Roi*, William III's path from Kensington Palace to St James's, verbally transformed into 'Rotten Row', has its loyal equestrians. The Serpentine, the curving stretch of water created in 1730 by damming the Westbourne Stream, is alive in summer with boats and bathers. Since the radical meetings held in Hyde Park in the unrestful 1840s the Sunday oratory of 'Speakers' Corner' where any and every subject is ventilated by all and sundry has been a continuing tradition.

The glades of Kensington Gardens, in effect an extension of Hyde Park though originally land belonging to Nottingham House, the property William III turned into Kensington Palace, lead to the City's western limit. A feature of the vista planned by the celebrated garden architect, Bridgeman, is the Round Pond, the bird-haunted water basin, seven acres in extent, where Shelley floated a paper boat and the youth of all ages at the present day launch their model ships.

The new City of Westminster incorporates nearly the whole of the largest and most countrified of London's parks, Regent's Park, grand design of John Nash in the time of the Prince Regent for the first and most luxurious of garden cities. The handsome terraces on its rim, in which Nash sought to combine the amenities of town house and country mansion, have been preserved, with some costly remodelling in recent times, in a way that guarantees their survival for a hundred years more. Nature and art are uniquely combined. The Broad Walk with its avenue of chestnut trees rivals that of Kensington Gardens. The ornamental water,

its islets providing nesting-places for rare water birds, curves round the Inner Circle in the same romantic fashion as at St James's Park though on a larger scale. The effect of spaciousness in Regent's Park, the sensation of country, is the more surprising in view of the many activities and diversions allowed for within its compass; the Zoological Gardens, the Open Air Theatre, the residence of the United States Ambassadors and Bedford College (formerly a women's college, but open to undergraduates of both sexes since 1965 and having some 1,000 students), as well as sports grounds for cricket, football, tennis, netball, hockey.

MONUMENTS AND LANDMARKS

So many are the reminders of historic events and great personalities in Westminster in the form of monuments and memorials that an account of them in full would occupy a whole volume. The sculptured memorials in the Abbey range in their extraordinary profusion from Queen Eleanor, wife of Edward I portrayed by the 13th-century London goldsmith, William Torel, to the Renaissance dignity of Torrigiani's tomb figures of Henry VII and his Queen, Elizabeth of York, and the theatrical brilliance of Roubiliac's Handel; while the wax images preserved in the Abbey's Undercroft Museum give a vividly life-like idea of the features of kings, queens and others of importance from the 14th to the 19th-century.

In its moving simplicity the Cenotaph in Whitehall designed by Sir Edwin Lutyens, the nation's memorial 'To The Glorious Dead', stands alone. The Gothic shrine of the Albert Memorial in Kensington Gardens, the grandiose Edwardian group of the Queen Victoria Memorial, however accessed as works of art, are the impressive symbols of a great age. By the garden wall of Marlborough House is Sir Alfred Gilbert's beautiful monument to Queen Alexandra. Often accounted the best of royal statues is the equestrian Charles I at Charing Cross by Le Sueur. From imposing columnar height, the Duke of York, son of George III, commands the way to the Mall at Waterloo Place. The heroes of war by land and sea have their due honour, Nelson on his column in Trafalgar Square, Wellington on his charger 'Copenhagen' in the monument at Hyde Park Corner, Nurse Cavell, martyr of the First World War, in St Martin's Place. Parliament Square has its assembly of statesmen—Canning, Peel, Disraeli, Abraham Lincoln in the craggy dignity of the replica of St Gaudens's statue at Chicago, Smuts by Epstein, alertly leaning forward. The statue of Cromwell by Hamo Thornycroft stands sombrely outside the Westminster Hall where once, after the Restoration, his severed head was exposed in ignominy.

Leicester Square assembles round its statue of Shakespeare the busts of the celebrities who lived thereabouts, the painters Reynolds and Hogarth, the surgeon Hunter and Sir Isaac Newton, whose house was in St

Martin's Street where the Westminster Central Reference Library is now situated. Gilbert and Sullivan of the Savoy Operas have their separate memorials appropriately within range of Savoy Hill, scene of their first success, along the Embankment; so too has the Embankment's engineer, Sir Joseph Bazalgette. The statue of the great actress Sarah Siddons, erected in 1897 on Paddington Green, near the old parish church of St Mary where she was buried in 1831, is of note on two accounts; in being the first open-air statue in London of a woman not of royal blood and also, it is supposed, the first of a member of the acting profession. There are many fascinating details in the Victorian open-air sculpture: the soldiers who stand guard by Wellington at Hyde Park Corner; the reliefs at the base of the Nelson Column; the *art nouveau* detail of the fountain beneath Sir Alfred Gilbert's aluminium *Eros* at Piccadilly Circus. Besides this much-loved figure there are many symbolic pieces of statuary that are essentially part of the London scene: 'Cleopatra's Needle', the Egyptian obelisk erected by Thothmes III at Heliopolis some 3,500 years ago, since 1878, flanked by Victorian sphinxes, a feature of the Embankment where by a sympathetic association of ideas the pavement seats are supported on cast-iron camels; Watts's *Physical Energy* in Kensington Gardens; Rodin's great *Burghers of Calais* in the Victoria Tower Gardens; Eric Gill's *Prospero and Ariel* at Broadcasting House; Adrian Jones's splendid Quadriga over the Arch at Constitution Hill; Epstein's *Virgin and Child* at the Convent of the Child Jesus in Cavendish Square. Of these and others the connoisseurs may compile a Westminster anthology to their own taste.

DIGNITY AND BEAUTY OF CHURCHES

A list of the places of worship which add to the dignity and beauty of Westminster in their design would be long. Completed in the early years of this century, the Catholic Westminster Cathedral, designed by John Francis Bentley, is a great conception in an Italo-Byzantine style, intended, as both Cardinal Manning and the architect agreed it should be, not to compete with the Abbey. Its campanile, 284 ft high, is an imposing landmark, its interior one of the most impressive in London in its vast simplicity – an austerity modified by marble facing, mosaics and Eric Gill's Stations of the Cross. The work of a succession of illustrious architects illustrates the change from late Gothic, of which the restored Savoy Chapel is a fragment, to the classical style, inaugurated by Inigo Jones in the Queen's Chapel, Marlborough Gate and St Paul's, Covent Garden. Sir Christopher Wren's only church in the West End except for St Anne's Soho (of which only the outer walls and tower, an early 19th-century addition, survived bombing in the Second World War), is St James's, Piccadilly. St James's was also heavily damaged in the Second World War but is now lavishly

restored. It contains the font by Grinling Gibbons that the diarist Evelyn so much admired. The Wren tradition has its exquisite continuance in the island churches that add so much character to the Strand, both sufferers from wartime damage now repaired.

St Clement Danes, a medieval foundation redesigned by Wren, with the addition of a graceful steeple by James Gibbs, now the church of the Royal Air Force, stands in partnership with St Mary-le-Strand, entirely the work of Gibbs, in which he again shows himself a master of the steeple. The statue of Dr Johnson in St Clement's tiny churchyard, a work of 1910, is a reminder of his attendance at services there when he repeated the responses in the Litany 'with tremendous energy'.

St George's, Hanover Square, designed by John James in the early 18th century, is notable for its portico of Corinthian columns, a feature adopted by Gibbs in the noble St Martin-in-the-Fields, its role as church of the royal parish of St Martin indicated by the royal arms on its pediment. Of the 19th-century return to medieval ideals the church of All Saints, Margaret Street, designed by William Butterfield, gives a striking instance in its elaborate richness of Victorian decoration, in fresco, marbles, carvings, mosaics and stained glass.

STREETS AND SQUARES

Planning in London has often been frustrated by its free and casual growth and Westminster in this respect is no exception, though two great architects have set their stamp upon it – Robert Adam and John Nash. The work of Adam has suffered much. The once beautiful riverside composition, the Adelphi Terrace, was a sad loss in the 1930s, though a few elegant buildings remain in the region leased by the three Adam brothers, the premises of the Royal Society of Arts among them. The development of the Portman Estate, north of Oxford Street, offered opportunities of which they made the most, though again in the course of time there have been many changes. A boulevard grandeur can be appreciated in Portland Place, though the consistency of its Adam houses has been sadly broken by later interpolations. Portman Square has decayed and been largely rebuilt. Yet there remain such gems of design as Robert Adam's Chandos House in Queen Anne Street and Home House, now the abode of the Courtauld Institute of Art in Portman Square.

The magnificence of John Nash's schemes extended from Regent's Park to Trafalgar Square (which was also his conception). He gave to Portland Place its graceful crescent at the northern end and made the Adam boulevard the first stage of his great thoroughfare southwards, hinged to the change of direction in Regent Street by the little circular church of All Souls. One can follow Nash along the curve of the rebuilt Regent Street Quadrant, see his handiwork in the façade of the Theatre Royal in the Haymarket, in still extant parts of his 'West Strand Improvements' and in the grandiose frontage of Carlton House Terrace on the Mall. But if these grand designs are fragmentary, Westminster has its full share of the typical features of London planning, squares and 'gardens'. Trafalgar Square and Leicester Square are in a special category, to be thought of in terms of sentiment rather than plan, Trafalgar Square especially as a magnet for all London's visitors and a place of public meetings and demonstrations. But of the square as a planned and originally residential enclosure Westminster has varied examples.

The first of the aristocratic West End squares, St James's, laid out in the later 17th century, retains an air of historic dignity. An Augustan harmony of ordered proportion remains in Queen Anne's Gate, which dates from 1704. The link-extinguishers of Grosvenor Square and Berkeley Square were long celebrated memories of the time when the torches of the link boys lit up the arrival of Georgian guests at the fashionable mansions though the associations of Grosvenor Square are now mainly of a later date and with the United States. The garden first planned by William Kent in the early 18th century is the setting for the statue of President Franklin D. Roosevelt, erected after the Second World War. The most distinctive feature of the square is the serrated façade in Portland stone and aluminium gilt of Saarinen's United States Embassy with its gilt eagle (blacked over in mourning when President Kennedy was assassinated).

Belgrave Square, princely in scale, marks the movement of fashion westwards after George III had made Buckingham House his palace. Development north of Oxford Street brought into being the elegant simplicity of Montagu and Bryanston Squares, both dating back to 1811 and continuing the Adam tradition. The transition from Regency to Victorian style can be studied in the region once called Tyburnia between Edgware Road and Westbourne Terrace and in such fine grouping as that presented by Hyde Park Gardens.

REGIONAL DIVERSITY

Much of Westminster is comprised in the 'West End' though in this area extending from Charing Cross to Hyde Park with Belgravia as its southern limit there is surprising variety. One may say broadly that the region to the east of Piccadilly Circus is 'theatreland'. The many theatres include the oldest of London's existing playhouses and – as rebuilt by Benjamin Wyatt in 1810-12 – the finest, the Drury Lane Theatre where Garrick, Kemble and Mrs Siddons once performed. Long its rival was the Royal Opera House where Handel first produced his *Messiah* in 1741, rebuilt in Covent Garden in 1858 and the present great centre of opera and ballet.

To the west in Piccadilly and St James's there is 'clubland'. The clubs of the late 18th century, White's,

Boodle's, Brooks's, line St James's Street. The United Services, the Athenaeum, the Travellers' and the Reform give classical and Italianate majesty to Pall Mall. Mayfair, north of Piccadilly and extending to Park Lane is in terms of architecture the legacy of the fashionable world of the 18th and 19th centuries though many mansions have been converted to professional and commercial use.

Regional diversity takes many forms. In Shepherd Market, Mayfair has one of those village-like oases that add so much to the special flavour of London. Soho is distinct from any other district, a foreign inner city enclosed by Oxford Street, Regent Street, Shaftesbury Avenue and Charing Cross Road, recruited since the 17th century by refugees from the conflicts of the Continent, a maze of alleys and byways, exotic in colour and character, contributing something to the legend of a 'swinging' London in the fashions promoted by Carnaby Street, Covent Garden, kitchen-garden ground of the monastery of Westminster in the Middle Ages, a fashionable promenade as laid out by Inigo Jones, a bustling spectacle of a morning when the porters hurry to and fro with their loads of fruit and vegetables, is as picturesque as when Hogarth painted it in his *Times of Day*. Picturesqueness of another kind may be found in the Paddington region popularly known by the name of 'Little Venice', where charming early Victorian houses terrace the Paddington Canal near where it widens at its junction with that remarkable waterway, the Regent's Canal. Robert Browning, who lived in Warwick Crescent, was one of those whom the scene poetically reminded of Venice.

Local character is also to be found in Westminster in its congregations of shops. In the Charing Cross Road one looks for old books; in Bond Street for the art dealers' galleries; in the 'ladies' mile' of Oxford Street for dress of every description; in St James's for those old-fashioned establishments that decree the minute but important changes in men's attire; in the arcades that branch off Piccadilly, the Burlington Arcade in particular, for all sorts of luxurious trinkets and haberdashery. The northern suburb of the augmented City, St John's Wood, in spite of widespread reconstruction, is still a region of artists' studios.

Apart from its theatres, concert halls, galleries and restaurants, Westminster has its several regional diversions. The river launches plying on the Thames afford a great panorama, especially those going downstream. They pass in succession: the York Watergate that in the 17th century gave access to the river from the Duke of Buckingham's mansion; the massive cubes of Shell-Mex House; Waterloo Bridge, the graceful lines of which lessen regret for the bridge by Sir John Rennie which it replaced; H.M.S. Discovery, the ship built to take Scott to the South Pole, now an R.N.V.R. training-vessel; and the river façade of Somerset House; before leaving Westminster behind en route for Greenwich. By water also one may gain an agreeably unconventional view of London by the boats that in summer run from Paddington's Little Venice, along the Regent's Canal as far as the Zoo. Not the least fascinating aspect of the Zoo itself is the way in which the needs and nature of its animal world have created special architectural forms, adding to Regency and Victorian design the Mappin Terraces of 1913 that dispensed with cages, the abstract-looking platforms of the Penguin Pool of the 1930s and Sir Hugh Casson's Elephant Pavilion and other buildings of the 1960s.

In the Marylebone region Madame Tussaud's waxworks exhibition, always under revision as new celebrities appear, has been a popular entertainment for more than 150 years; while the dome of the Planetarium, built on the site of the bombed Tussaud cinema, gives its scientific presentation of celestial space. Those who vainly look in Baker Street for Sherlock Holmes's fictional address, 221B, may find its interior reconstructed in the Sherlock Holmes Tavern in Northumberland Street, faithful to Conan Doyle's description in every detail, the unanswered correspondence affixed to the mantelpiece with a jack-knife, the tobacco in a Persian slipper and the initials V.R. on the wall picked out with bullet-holes.

CENTRES OF THE ARTS, LEARNING AND SCIENCE

There are fabulous treasures of art in Westminster. The unique collection of masterpieces in the National Gallery has been enriched by many acquisitions in recent years, including the great *Virgin and St Anne* of Leonardo. The Tate Gallery has been completely rehung since 1967 and gives both an historical survey of British art and a view of all that is most modern in painting and sculpture. The National Portrait Gallery, the Wallace Collection at Hertford House, greatest of private art gifts to the nation, the Wellington Museum at Apsley House, the Queen's Gallery at Buckingham Palace, which regularly places on show some aspect of the royal collection, are all in the City of Westminster. Here also is the world's central art market. At Sotheby's in Bond Street and Christie's in King Street, auction-room history is made in the international competition for works by masters old and modern, for art of every kind. Here too are the headquarters of the art societies, the Royal Institute of British Architects in Portland Place, the Royal Academy at Burlington House, the Federation of British Artists in Suffolk Place, the Institute of Contemporary Arts and other societies at Carlton House Terrace. From Westminster operate the organisations that support national effort and uphold standards in the arts; the Arts Council, the Council of Industrial Design, with its shop window in the Design Centre in the Haymarket, the Crafts Centre. The Royal College of Art, now raised to university status, includes in its sphere every aspect and function of design. The Courtauld Institute of Art is the training ground of art scholarship.

Music is served by the Royal Academy of Music in Marylebone Road, which gained its royal charter in 1830. The giant amphitheatre of the Royal Albert Hall is the supremely dramatic setting of musical performance. In the London Library there is one of the more important instruments of learning and research that in Westminster supplement the British Museum Library. In a part of London where the first printing-press and publishing house in England was set up by William Caxton at the Abbey, about 1471, it is of interest to note that the first rate-supported public library in London was established in Great Smith Street in 1857; The City now has one of the most extensive and best-supplied library systems in the country. Science in the broadest sense is represented by the great 17th-century foundation, the Royal Society, accommodated since 1967 in premises in Carlton House Terrace affording more than twice the space the Society previously had at Burlington House. Within the western boundary where Westminster adjoins the complex of Kensington museums is the Imperial College of Science and Technology, equipped as the main spearhead of higher technological education.

DYNAMIC CITY OF TODAY

Westminster, with all its historic memories and buildings, is dynamically modern. Broadcasting House is the administrative centre of the widely spreading network of radio and television. Every great air line and shipping line has its office within a short radius of Piccadilly Circus. At Bush House and along the Strand the London headquarters of the Commonwealth countries are concentrated. The skyline changes rapidly and constantly as the tall new buildings, apartments, office blocks, hotels, come into being. Victoria Street, once so essentially Victorian, is a brand-new thoroughfare where the Westminster City Council occupies a 20-storey building. The Vickers Building dwarfs the neighbouring Tate Gallery. The tower of flats of Kemp House soars above the stalls of the old street market in Berwick Street, Soho.

Modern planning takes many forms. One of the largest and most attractively varied housing estates of recent times is Churchill Gardens on Grosvenor Road. The widening Strand has a new architectural key in the distinguished Peter Robinson store. Underground, the new Victoria Line will create a fresh link from north to south with Victoria Station, the 'gateway to Europe'. Underpasses and fly-overs like that of Harrow Road foreshadow the City of the future. 'Ships, towers, domes, theatres and temples', the prospect that inspired Wordsworth in the immortal sonnet composed upon Westminster Bridge, has, in the second half of the 20th century, a newly inspiring extension.

THE COAT OF ARMS *(1)* of the City of Westminster
outside its new City Hall in Victoria Street is cast in aluminium coloured with stove enamel, the background being of
black granite. The designer was W. J. G. Verco, M.V.O.

ROYAL ABBEY *(2, 3)*: Although a church may have stood on wild Thorney Island at least as early as the eighth century, Edward the Confessor, more a monk than a king, is regarded as the founder of Westminster Abbey, and there he has a shrine. He built the place grandly in the eleventh century in solid Norman manner, and added a palace for himself close by. So began that association of the Abbey with the Monarchy which made Westminster the traditional centre of Court, Government and Law. In 1560 Elizabeth I turned the Abbey into a collegiate church and so it has remained. The thirteenth-century vaulting of the nave, *2*, is unusually high for an English church. The church, *3*, seen across Dean's Yard with its mediaeval flying buttresses and its two eighteenth-century towers.

ROYAL ABBEY (4-7): The extension to the east begun by Henry VII as a Lady Chapel in 1503, and completed by Henry VIII some nine years later as Henry VII's Chantry Chapel, is a fine flower of the final phase of Gothic engineering in stone. The cobweb of fan-vaulting, 7, which roofs the Chapel. The exterior of the Chapel, 4, with its five smaller radiating chapels on the east, its buttressing turrets and 'its nice, embroidered work', as Wren described it.

The vault of the Abbey's Chapter House, 5, although re-built in the nineteenth century on the thirteenth century walls, still indicates the original beauty of this octagonal council chamber where Parliament often met in the Middle Ages. The fourteenth-century moated Jewel House, 6, to the south-west of the Abbey was built like a miniature castle to protect the valuables of Edward III.

FACES IN THE ABBEY *(8-15)*: The church is crowded in its haphazard hundreds with the tombs, monuments and effigies designed for the changing tastes of seven centuries. Here is a random selection of the heads to be found among them, including four from that remarkable miniature Madame Tussaud's Exhibition in the Crypt displaying death-masks and wax images which reveal how the royal and the renowned really looked. *8*, Henry VII (Is this the face of a murderer?). *9*, Elizabeth of York (d.1503). *10*, Anne of Bohemia (d.1394). *11*, Charles II (d.1685). (Those four are in the Crypt.) *12*, William Wilberforce in the north aisle by S. Joseph, 1840. A chubby angel, *13*, on the famous tomb of Henry VII by Torrigiani, 1518. The calm and formalised effigy, *14*, of Edward III (d.1377) in gilded bronze. *15*, Elizabeth I carved in 1606 by Maximilian Colt.

ROYAL PALACES *(16, 17)*: London's first royal palace stood near the river, forming a single complex with the Abbey. Finally Henry VIII moved it slightly to the north and soon it was so large and rambling that it extended right up Whitehall to Charing Cross. He also built St James's Palace. Buckingham House did not become a royal residence until the 1820s, when John Nash reconstructed it as part of his metropolitan improvements. In spite of its present stone face and frontal approaches built in *beaux arts* style by Sir Aston Webb around 1913, the Palace with its lawns, trees, lake and stable wing retains something of the character of a large English country house. Much of Nash's work remains. *16*, a detail of the florid memorial to Queen Victoria which stands in front of the Palace at the end of the Mall, was sculptured by Sir Thomas Brock and erected in 1901. It is often despised today, but it has the merits of confidence and skill. *17*, the colourful morning ritual of the Changing of the Guard in the forecourt of the Palace always attracts a crowd.

ROYAL PALACES *(18-20)*: Only parts of the original Palace of St James built by Henry VIII remain. The arcade in Ambassadors' Court, *18,* where a red-coated guard stands on sentry duty, is of later date. One of the few traces of Henry VIII's Palace of Whitehall which survived the fire of 1698 is the brick wine cellar, *19.* This was originated by Cardinal Wolsey and its east wall is, in fact, mediaeval. During the building of the new Ministry of Defence the whole cellar, weighing 4,000 tons, was moved with rollers and jacks to its present position below its original one at ground level. The brick stillages once supported great barrels of wine. The top of the original gatehouse of St James's Palace is here seen, *20,* against the framework of a new office tower of the kind which is changing London's skyline.

NATIONAL GOVERNMENT (21-23): Most of the squalid jumble in which the Government of an Empire had been housed for too long was burned down in 1834 – to everyone's relief. Happily the splendid Great Hall with its hammer-beam roof, which Richard II had rebuilt in the fourteenth century, was saved and was incorporated in the new building of the Palace of Westminster we see today. Erected between 1837 and 1857 to designs by Sir Charles Barry with lavish decorations by Augustus Pugin, this is one of the best examples of Gothic Revival anywhere in the world, not least in its clear and classical planning. With its many towers, turrets and spires the building provides one of London's nodal points with what the capital too often lacks elsewhere: an interesting skyline. A typical roofscape of the building, 21, above and around the Lobby seen from the west. The Clock Tower, 22, enclosing the great cracked bell of Big Ben seen from the east end of Westminster Bridge, where a lion of Coade stone, which once surmounted a riverside brewery near by, guards the approach to the City. The silhouette of the Houses of Parliament, 23, can be seen at its romantic best when dusk is falling.

WHITEHALL *(24):* The view looking north towards Trafalgar Square and away from Parliament Square. In 1530 Henry VIII took over the Palace of York from Cardinal Wolsey and, adding to it greatly, called it White-hall. Today the street is mainly composed of the head-quarters of government departments and of the Forces. On

the left is the Ionic portico of Dover House which was built in the eighteenth century as a private residence but has been occupied since 1885 by the Scottish Office. Beyond it are the Horse Guards, the Paymaster General's Office and the old Admiralty Building with its Screen. In the distance Nelson's Column forms a climax to the vista.

NATIONAL GOVERNMENT *(25, 26)*: The entrance rotunda of Dover House, *25*, with its Tuscan columns and its glazed dome, was designed by Henry Holland in the 1780s. It stands on a site once occupied by Henry VIII's open tennis court, the gallery of his Tilt Yard and one end of an ornate gateway said to have been designed by Holbein. No. 10 Downing Street, *26*, the official residence of the Prime Minister, stands in a little street off Whitehall. Here a small quiet group is always gathered and sometimes a large and rowdy one. Its front, refaced in 1766, is a typically unpretentious example of London's eighteenth-century domestic architecture. But its front is deceptive for behind it lies a warren of rooms, in one of which the Cabinet meets; it also connects with Nos. 11 and 12, while somewhere at the rear is a walled garden.

THE LAW *(27, 28)*: In 1225 the Law Courts were fixed near the Palace of Westminster where the King lived at the country's administrative and judicial centre. When Henry VIII moved to Whitehall the Law Courts remained in a cluster around and within the Great Hall. There they stayed until 1882, when they were moved to, *27,* a new building in the Strand. It was designed by G. E. Street in a thirteenth-century style with its own Great Hall 230 feet long. As an example of High Victorian Gothic, it has merit, not least in the free composition of its Strand elevation seen here. In the name of efficiency the Police Headquarters in London were moved in 1967 from their familiar building on the Victoria Embankment to, *28,* a modern one in Broadway, off Victoria Street (by Chapman, Taylor and Partners). It makes an impersonal contrast to Street's ebullient design but retains the name New Scotland Yard to provide romantic overtones.

THE LAW *(29-31)*: Somerset House in the Strand is associated with the Law in containing a number of public offices, including the General and Probate Registries. It is, in fact, not only London's but the world's first great metropolitan office block. Built of Portland stone, it was begun in 1776 to the designs of Sir William Chambers, the Surveyor General who also designed the Pagoda in Kew Gardens. Its purpose was to house such offices as those of the Navy, Ordnance, Exchequer, Taxes, Audit, Privy Seal and, for a time, the Royal Academy, the Royal Society and the Society of Antiquaries, as well as to serve as an appropriate symbol of a powerful nation. It surrounds a large central quadrangle flanked by two smaller courts, and before the Victoria Embankment was built the Thames lapped its south arcade. The west end at the approach to Waterloo Bridge, *29*, was designed by Sir James Pennethorne. Although built as late as 1856 it conforms well with the academic classicism of the rest of the building. Within it toil officials of the Board of Inland Revenue. A keystone, *30*, in the quadrangle, one of its many excellent carvings. *31*, Somerset House seen beyond Waterloo Bridge from the south bank of the river.

KING AND PARLIAMENT (*32-35*): The most famous building in Whitehall is, *32*, the Banqueting Hall, here seen from the portico of Dover House. Designed by Inigo Jones in the classical and learned style of Palladio, it was the first Renaissance building in London. As such it must have seemed a dramatic innovation to the untravelled Londoner of the seventeenth century, not least in its unfamiliar use of Portland stone. Built for James I, 'King of Great Britain', as the centre of a new palace which was never to be consummated, it was more than a dining hall; it was also a symbol of divine kingship. There royal banquets appealed to all the senses, and feasting was combined with music, masques

and rose-scented air until the Puritans laid their blight on the land and Charles I emerged one day in 1649 from the central window of the Hall on to a scaffold. The bronze statue, *33*, of Charles the Martyr at the north end of Whitehall (by Hubert Le Sueur, 1633) is the City's finest equestrian statue. The statue of Cromwell *34*, by the Great Hall of Westminster Palace, was made by Sir William Thornycroft in 1899. A detail, *35*, from one of the ceiling panels by Rubens commissioned by Charles I and completed in 1634. The general subject is the Apotheosis of James I and this panel represents the Union of England and Scotland with Minerva holding a crown over the infant.

THE NAVY *(36, 37)*: Although Nelson's tomb is in St Paul's Cathedral, the hero of Trafalgar can be seen, *36*, as though in the flesh among the figures in the Crypt of Westminster Abbey. His likeness can also be seen, though only in distant silhouette, *37*, on the top of his Corinthian column in the centre of Trafalgar Square 145 feet above the crowds. Here it is glimpsed from the portico of the National Gallery. The statue, 17 feet high, is by E. H. Baily. The Monument, built in 1842, is better known, however, for the four affectionate lions of bronze guarding its base, which often serves as a provisional platform for open-air speakers. The lions were the work of the Victorian artist Sir Edwin Landseer and were completed in 1857. The square, which did not acquire its name until 1830, was another town-planning idea which came from the fertile mind of John Nash.

THE NAVY *(38-40)*: The offices of the Admiralty stand near Trafalgar Square, the older buildings being towards the north end of Whitehall. The Admiralty Screen of 1761 designed by Robert Adam in his youth, *38*, adds interest to the building behind designed by Thomas Ripley in 1726. That building served originally as residences for the Lords of the Admiralty, the Board Room, (still used for naval conferences) being the only office. The magnificent carving of garlands and nautical emblems surrounding an eight-eenth-century wind-compass, *39*, which decorates the Board Room fireplace is believed to be by Grinling Gibbons. Together with the rest of the panelling and decorations it was probably retained from the earlier building which stood on the site. *40*, St Martin-in-the-Fields with its attrac-tive spire, seen here from the portico of the National Gallery, is well sited to the north-east of Trafalgar Square. Built by James Gibbs in the 1720s, it has come to be regarded as the Navy's special church.

23ʳᵈ ROYAL WELSH FUSILIERS

THE ARMY *(41-44)*: This is well represented in the City of Westminster by the War Office in Whitehall, the Horse Guards facing it, by Wellington, Chelsea and Knightsbridge Barracks and a number of monuments. Two of the four bronze soldiers on the Duke of Wellington's statue at Hyde Park Corner, *41*, which faces Apsley House, *89*, where the Duke lived – a competent work of 1888 by Sir Joseph Boehm. The Horse Guards in Whitehall was designed in the 1740s by William Kent (a reviver of the Palladian style under Lord Burlington), but it was not erected until the 1750s, after his death. It is a tourist attraction not only as a lively piece of period architecture but on account of its colourful daily pageantry when the Guards are changed. The Whitehall front, *42* and *43*, the elevation seen from an entrance to St James's Park across the Horse Guards' Parade where the royal and impressive ceremony of Trooping the Colour takes place once a year. Overleaf, *44*, the Changing of the Guard at the Horse Guards.

THE ROYAL AIR FORCE *(45)*: Being of recent formation, the R.A.F. has few associations or monuments in Westminster, although it has its headquarters in the new Ministry of Defence in Whitehall. However, the old church of St Clement Danes, with a foundation probably going back at least a thousand years, has been dedicated to the Force. The body of the Church, which stands on an island at the east end of the Strand, was designed by Wren in the 1680s, but this was bombed in the Second World War and has since been rebuilt. The graceful spire built by James Gibbs in 1719 survives.

FOREIGN AFFAIRS *(46)*: Part of the façade of the Foreign Office facing St James's Park. The building stretches like a vast Italian palace of the fifteenth century right back to Parliament Street at the southern end of Whitehall and from King Charles Street to Downing Street. This competent example of High Victorianism is by Sir George Gilbert Scott, who was more often on the side of the Gothic faction in the battle of the styles.

FOREIGN AND COMMONWEALTH AFFAIRS *(47-49)*: The most imposing Embassy in London is that of the U.S.A., *47*, which occupies the whole west side of that Little America called Grosvenor Square. Built in the 1960s by the Finnish architect, Eero Saarinen, it is topped by Old Baldy, the American Eagle. The architecture of the Commonwealth buildings in Westminster is less impressive. *48*, South Africa House seen to the east across Trafalgar Square is by Sir Herbert Baker and belongs to the 1930s. On the opposite side of the Square stands Canada·House, *49*. This building originally formed part of a dignified structure in Bath stone by Sir Robert Smirke designed for the Union Club and the Royal College of Physicians in the 1820s, but it has since been debased. In the distance along Cockspur Street can be seen the modern New Zealand House at the south end of Haymarket. It is the work of Sir Robert Matthew, Marshall and Johnson and was completed in 1962. Australia House is some distance away in the Strand.

LOCAL GOVERNMENT *(50, 51)*: Facing Parliament Square on the west, *50*, stands the Middlesex Guildhall containing court rooms – an eccentric building of 1905 by Gibson and Russell in mediaeval *art nouveau* lavishly decorated with sculpture by H. C. Fehr. By contrast, *51*, the new Westminster City Hall in Victoria Street. The building, by Sir John Burnet, Tait and Partners, was not designed specifically as a town hall but as a general office block. It has since been adapted. It is an uncompromising utility structure of the 'sixties without decoration except for the coat of arms by the entrance. However, it does provide the accommodation needed for administering an area which was so greatly enlarged in 1965.

CHURCHES *(52-60)*: The City of Westminster contains centres of worship for many religions and denominations. Those of the established Church are, of course, the most numerous and on the whole the best architecturally. The charming domed tower with its golden angels, *52*, of the parish church of St Mary in Marylebone Road (Thomas Hardwick, 1813). The Methodists' Central Hall, Storey's Gate, *53*, is very French in a *beaux arts* manner (Lanchester and Rickards, 1911). Two of the four towers of Baroque St John's, Smith Square, *54*, which was a casualty of war (Thomas Archer, 1728). The dominating Byzantine campanile, *55*, of the Catholic Cathedral in Ashley Place (J. F. Bentley, 1903). St Paul, Covent Garden, *56*, (Inigo Jones 1613, rebuilt by Hardwick after 1795). St Margaret, *57*, standing in the shade of the Abbey north of Henry VII's Chapel is of twelfth-century foundation (1523 but much altered since). St John's Wood Chapel, *58*, (Hardwick, 1813). St George, Hanover Square, *59*, (John James, 1724). The front of St Mary, Marylebone Road, *60*. Not shown, but worth noting, is St Augustine, Kilburn, by J. L. Pearson, for in its spatial composition it is one of the finest Victorian churches in the country.

CHURCHES *(61, 62)*: St Mary-le-Strand was built in 1717 under Queen Anne's Act for Fifty New Churches, the architect being James Gibbs. It stands on a traffic island and so its beauty can be clearly seen from all sides, 'as if it were a casket one can handle with one's hands', to quote Dr Pevsner. This civilised little building, *61*, its Portland stone gleaming white in the sunshine, is here seen from the west at the Strand entrance to Somerset House. (In the distance rises the spire of St Clement Danes, also by Gibbs). The plain interior has a covered and richly coffered ceiling, *62*, inspired by the churches of SS Apostoli and SS Luca e Martina in Rome.

THE ARTS *(63-65)*: On the north side of Trafalgar Square stands the National Gallery, *63*, where the nation's finest public collection of paintings is housed. The building was completed in 1838 to designs by William Wilkins with a central portico surmounted by a dome. The interior is Victorian. The Albert Hall, *64*, here seen from the Albert Memorial, is an international centre for large gatherings but is used mainly as a concert hall. It is the dominating and most northerly building of an area laid out for learning from the profits of the 1851 Great Exhibition. Built in the 1870s to the design of Captain Fowke, R.E., its great oval, like a Roman amphitheatre, is 735 feet in circumference and can seat 8,000 people. The steps of the Tate Gallery, *65*, are adorned with a bronze by Renoir. The building itself, standing on the site of a huge, and ill-famed penitentiary, is of classic style and was built in 1897 as a gift from Sir Henry Tate, the sugar magnate, the architect being Sidney Smith. The Gallery is concerned mainly with modern painting and sculpture.

THE ARTS *(66-68)*: London has many theatres but only a few have architectural distinction. Among the few is the Theatre Royal, Haymarket, *66*, which was founded in 1720 and has a front of 1821 by John Nash. In typical Nash manner, it lies monumentally on the axis from St James's Square along Charles Street. The interior of the Royal Opera House, Covent Garden, *67*, is by E. M. Barry, a successful Victorian architect and son of Sir Charles Barry, who designed among other things, the Charing Cross Hotel, part of the inside of the National Gallery and the Floral Hall of Covent Garden Market (see *100*). The noble Rotunda of Drury Lane, *68*, is one of the original remaining parts of London's finest theatre, built in 1812 by Benjamin Wyatt.

GEORGE FREDERICK HANDEL Esq.
born February XXIII. MDCLXXXIV.
died April XIV. MDCCLIX.

L.F.Roubiliac invᵗ et s

THE ARTS *(69-73)*: Creative talent is well represented among the statues of Westminster – not least in the Poets' Corner of the south transept of the Abbey. There can be seen among others John Dryden by Scheemakers, Ben Jonson by Rysbrack, John Milton also by Rysbrack, Dr Johnson by Nollekens, Shakespeare by Scheemakers and, *69*, Handel by Roubiliac, a fine carving of 1761. Outdoor pieces include, *70*, Robert Burns, a bronze of 1884 in the Embankment Gardens by Sir John Steell – Sarah Siddons, the great eighteenth-century actress, *71*, depicted in an inept but not unattractive carving of 1897 by Chavalliaud at Paddington Green – the bust of Sir Christopher Wren, *72*, at the Headquarters of the Royal Institute of British Architects in Portland Place, a seventeenth-century version of the one in the Ashmolean Museum, Oxford, by Edward Pearce – the bronze head of William Blake, *73*, by Sir Jacob Epstein in Poets' Corner.

EDUCATION *(74-77)*: *74*, the Greycoat School in Greycoat Place, founded 1701. Badly damaged in World War II, it has been restored in Queen Anne style. The Charity Children of wood are early 18th-century. *75*, the Bluecoat School in Caxton Street, founded 1709. In the niche is a Charity Boy. *76*, a new building of the Imperial College of Science and Technology, Exhibition Road, an area developed in its present form after the Great Exhibition. *77*, the lantern and ceiling above the staircase of Ashburnham House. A stately home in the 1660s, it now holds the Westminster School library. The architect may have been John Webb, nephew of Inigo Jones.

THE PARKS *(78, overleaf)*: All the major parks of inner London lie within Westminster. The famous view across the lake of St James's Park towards the cluster of buildings of Whitehall and beyond with their dreamlike but unpremeditated composition – the Horse Guards, the War Office and the distant roofs of Whitehall Court. The Park was a swamp until Henry VIII drained the area to make a deer park for his new St James's Palace.

THE PARKS *(79-81)*: A wintry scene, *79*, across the lake of St James's Park looking towards the Foreign Office. The lake in Regent's Park, *80*, with the Regency villa, The Holme, designed by Decimus Burton about 1818. With its surrounding terraces of stucco houses and its scattered villas, the Park (at first named Marylebone Park) was laid out by John Nash in the 1810s as an early Garden City and a picturesque culmination to his town planning scheme extending north from the Mall by way of Regent Street to the Park. The east end of the Serpentine lake in Hyde Park, *81*, has a new café pavilion designed with a fantasy too rare in modern design. This park was Abbey land until Henry VIII enclosed it for hunting deer.

THE ZOO *(82-84)*: The Zoological Gardens were laid out in 1827 by Decimus Burton to the north of Regent's Park. Through the Gardens runs a pound of the Grand Union Canal, called the Regent's Canal, which Nash applied as a decorative element in his landscaping. The new Aviary, 1965, *82*, designed by Lord Snowdon, Cedric Price and Frank Newby, rises above the Canal. The new Elephant House, *83*, was designed by Casson, Conder and Partners. The Penguin Pool, *84*, is one of the revolutionary but distinguished structures of the 1930s designed by the firm of Tecton.

NASH'S GRAND PLAN *(85-87)*: With the support of the Prince Regent, John Nash did much in his histrionic way to give central London whatever form and monumentality it now possesses, notably in his spinal Triumphal Way, which, though debased, still runs from the Mall across Piccadilly Circus, up to Regent Street and Portland Place to Park Crescent and Regent's Park. Park Crescent, *85*, (previous page) formed in conjunction with Park Square to its north, the climax of Nash's *Via Triumphalis* where it enters Regent's Park. Like much of Nash's other work, these houses were faced with stucco intended to represent stone and, though dramatic in their total effect and designed for Carriage Folk, they were often jerry-built. A change of direction occurs where Upper Regent Street joins Portland Place. There Nash brilliantly solved the visual problem by designing, *86*, the circular porch with its pencil point spire of All Souls' Church in Langham Place. The Duke of York's Monument and Carlton House Terrace, *87*, here seen from the Mall, were built by Nash when the Regent's residence, Carlton House, was demolished in 1829. The monument by Benjamin Wyatt with its bronze statue by Richard Westmacott was erected in 1833.

Pedestrian
Subway

Hyde Park Corner
Station
Hyde Park
Knightsbridge
CONVENIENCES

HOMES OLD AND NEW (*88*, on previous page): Three generations of houses in Pimlico: Dolphin Square at the back, a huge block of flats built in the 1930s around a courtyard to a design by Gordon Jeeves – a terrace of stucco houses remaining from the residential district built by Thomas Cubitt in the areas of Belgravia and Pimlico in the 1830s and 1840s – and, in the foreground, part of the large housing scheme of Churchill Gardens built since the War for Westminster City Council by Powell and Moya.

HOMES OLD AND NEW (*89-91*): Apsley House at Hyde Park Corner, *89*, otherwise called No. 1 Piccadilly, was built in the 1770s by Robert Adam for Baron Apsley. In 1829 the Duke of Wellington bought it and then Benjamin and Philip Wyatt altered it. It is now the Wellington Museum. Eaton Square, *90*, is one of the impressive classical terraces of Belgravia erected as an aristocratic quarter by the speculative builder, Thomas Cubitt, in the 1830s and 1840s. Part of the new local authority housing, *91*, near the Harrow Road in the northerly part of the City, symbolises England's twentieth-century social revolution.

HOMES OLD AND NEW *(92-96)*: Some old domestic details of Westminster, including four doorways. *92*, Queen Anne's Gate. *93*, Queen Anne Street. *94*, the Adelphi. *95*, Dean's Yard. The Staircase of 1744 at No. 44 Berkeley Square, *96*, by William Kent is the finest of its kind London offers. Though confined in a fairly small space, the staircase has grandeur. The house was built as a private dwelling but it now shelters the world's most exclusive gaming club.

HOMES OLD AND NEW *(97-99):* A strong contrast in architectural expression can be found in St James's Place, here seen from the east side of the Green Park. On the left, *97*, are the modern luxury flats by Denys Lasdun, and on the right is Spencer House, a noble mansion of the 1760s by John Vardy. A remnant of the speculative riverside housing scheme, designed and promoted by the Adam brothers in the 1770s and called the Adelphi, is No. 7 Adam Street, *98*, now the offices of the medical magazine, *The Lancet.* Queen Anne's Gate, *99*, with its exceptional early eighteenth-century houses at its west end.

COMMERCE LARGE AND SMALL *(100):* Covent Garden is London's main market for fruit and vegetables, appropriately so because here in the Middle Ages lay the vegetable garden of Westminster Abbey. In the seventeenth century the area was developed by Inigo Jones for the Duke of Bedford as London's first square having arcaded houses around it and the Church of St Paul on its west side. Being based on an Italian idea it was called the Piazza.

COMMERCE LARGE AND SMALL *(101-105)*: The hat shop, *101*, of the early eighteenth century in St James's Street. A small store, *102*, at the corner of a Victorian tenement block in the depths of Westminster purveys immediate household needs including local gossip. Burlington Arcade, *103*, off Piccadilly, the covered pedestrian way for West End luxury shopping, was built in 1819 by Samuel Ware. The famous auction room of Sotheby's, *104*, in Bond Street. In contrast to small enterprise, *105*, is the Millbank Tower occupied by the Vickers engineering group, the Ministry of Technology and others, the architects being Ronald Ward and Partners. In the foreground the front of the Tate Gallery provides a relieving foil with its hand-wrought stonework.

HOSTELS LARGE AND SMALL *(106, 107)*: One of the latest luxury hotels in the City is, *106*, the Hilton. The hotel, opened in 1963, was designed by Lewis Solomon, Kaye and Partners with William Tabler of New York as consultant. It overlooks Hyde Park across Park Lane and is here seen from Hyde Park Corner. A typical London pub, *107*, with its engraved Victorian glass: the Champion in Wells Street.

CLUBLAND *(108, 109):* Along St James's Street and Pall Mall and around Waterloo Place stand most of London's famous clubs. The institution of the Club, exclusive to professional and upper-class males, often astonishes the foreign visitor. It has a long tradition which began over two centuries ago when the Club replaced the more democratic Coffee House. There the gentry could talk politics or gamble away their fortunes. Many are architecturally distinguished like, *108,* Boodle's in St James's Street built in 1765 by J. Crunden in an Adam-like way. Another is the Travellers' built in 1832 in an Italian Renaissance style by Sir Charles Barry, architect of the Houses of Parliament. Its peaceful library, *109,* has a frieze cast from an ancient classical building.

ARCHES OF WESTMINSTER *(110-112):* The most famous of these, *110,* is Marble Arch – particularly as a landmark where Park Lane, Oxford Street, Edgware Road and Bayswater Road conjoin. It was designed by John Nash in 1828 to serve as a gateway to the forecourt of Buckingham Palace but was moved to its present position in 1851. It is indeed faced with marble, its inspiration being the Arch of Constantine. Admiralty Arch, *111,* at the east end of the Mall was built in a grandiose Edwardian way by Sir Aston Webb in 1911 to form part of the monumental scheme connected with his refronting of Buckingham Palace. Constitution Arch, *112,* at Hyde Park Corner is by Decimus Burton. It was erected in 1846 on an axis with his neighbouring Screen at the entrance to Hyde Park, but it was moved to its present site at the top of Constitution Hill in 1883. At first it supported a gigantic equestrian statue of Wellington but that was replaced in 1912 by the present bronze *Victory* by Adrian Jones.

DETAILS IN STONE (113-118): One of the pleasures of exploring any large city is to search for its decorative details. The cartouche, 113, in the east pediment of St Martin-in-the-Fields. A plaque, 114, by the Danish-born Michael Spang on Robert Adam's Admiralty Screen in Whitehall. Two of the three fallen women, 115, who grace the terrace of a modern office block off the Strand. A father figure, 116, gazes sternly across Parliament Square. *Day* by Jacob Epstein, 117, on the headquarters of the London Passenger Transport Board in Broadway. *Asia* by J. H. Foley, 118, one of the four corner groups adorning Sir George Gilbert Scott's Albert Memorial.

DETAILS IN BRONZE *(119-125)*: The statue of *Victory* by Adrian Jones, *119*, which tops the Constitution Arch at Hyde Park Corner. Boudicca, or Boadicea, Queen of the Iceni made by Thomas Thornycroft in 1850, *120*, continues to resist the Roman invaders in her chariot at Westminster Bridge. A detail of Rodin's masterly *Burghers of Calais*, *121*, in Victoria Tower Gardens. *Physical Energy* by G. F. Watts, *122*, in Kensington Gardens. The statue of James II, *123*, made by Grinling Gibbons in 1686. One of the pair of Sphinxes by George Vulliamy, *124*, which guard Cleopatra's Needle on Victoria Embankment. Prince Albert within his shrine, *125*, holds a copy of the Catalogue of the Great Exhibition in his hand – a fine piece of craftsmanship by J. H. Foley.

DETAILS IN IRON *(126-135)*: Three iron lamp-posts, *126-128*: a rich Victorian casting in Trafalgar Square, a dolphin design on Victoria Embankment and a George IV piece in York Gate near Regent's Park. Three bollasters, *129-131*: a George IV relic near Regent's Park, a modern example in Churchill Gardens, and an eccentric personage off Downing Street. Three coal-hole covers or Opercula, *132-134*, symbolise the fog-wrapped city of Dickens's day. Old castings are growing rare but Montagu Square still possesses a particularly varied collection from which these are selected. One of the pair of bronze-coated cast-iron gates, *135*, of Constitution Arch with its Royal coat of arms.

LINES OF COMMUNICATION *(136, 137)*: Since the Roman Occupation London has remained the country's main centre of government, trade and culture as well as its largest port. Towards London all main lines of transport have always converged and within the City of Westminster itself now run London's chief road arteries – at least two of which are of Roman origin. The Mall, *136*, seen here from Queen Victoria's Monument in front of Buckingham Palace is a wide ceremonial way ending at Admiralty Arch and is of fairly recent foundation. Charles II first laid it out in the 1660s with four rows of trees as part of a new landscaping of St James's Park, but its character has since been altered – first by Nash's Carlton House Terrace on the north side and later by Webb's works. An iron arch, *137*, of one of London's great covered railway termini: Paddington Station built by I. K. Brunel in the 1850s at the start of his Great Western Railway.

LINES OF COMMUNICATION *(138-143)*: Although the canals centred on Birmingham and the industrial Midlands, London was linked with the national network by the Grand Junction Canal. Now called the Grand Union, it runs across the north of the City to the river and its great port, and is here seen, *138*, in the district called Little Venice. But the Thames has always been and still remains London's chief line of communication and its chief reason for existence ever since the Romans built a bridge there in almost the same spot where London Bridge stands today. Above are a few riverside objects along the Victoria Em-

bankment. The York Water Gate of 1626 in the Embankment Gardens, *139*, which once served as a landing stage to the garden of the Duke of Buckingham's mansion (one of many grand houses which once faced the river along the Strand). The river lapped the Gate until Sir Joseph Bazalgette built his impressive granite-faced Embankment in the 1860s. An original seat with sphinxes, *140*. The bust of Bazalgette, *141*, below Hungerford Bridge. A lamp-post dolphin of cast iron, *142*. Overleaf, *143*, Captain Scott's ship *Discovery* now preserved beside the Embankment as a national symbol for a maritime race.